Molding A Man

Book I

Molding/Making A Woman

Homemaker, Wife, Mother

Orature

Richard J. Bias

Molding A Man, Book I: Molding/Making A Woman
Homemaker, Wife, Mother—Orature
Copyright © 2023 by Richard J. Bias

Paperback: 978-1959151944
e-book: 978-1959151951

The Reading Glass
BOOKS

The Reading Glass Books
1-800-608-6550
www.readingglassbooks.com
production@readingglassbooks.com

<u>Dedication:</u>

This Book is dedicated to my Mother Inez L. Bias, and all the women in my immediate family my sister's, extended family the Wells sisters, and all the women confidantes who help guide me through life. Being around amazing women and seeing the greatness in them inspired me to write this book. It's supposed to give the readers the information to guide the women in her circle. It should give each woman her own identity and the things she needs to be a great woman. My hope is at the completion of this book each woman will fine the skills to not only continue to inspire herself but also inspire other women around her. This Orature was edited by Eric Miller.

Preview:

Thought-out history the world has been nurtured from the hard work of inspired women within each society. Nothing is more amazing than a woman who can create a great woman with her hands and mind. Building a Home from the shell of a house to become one of the world's wonders. The home is the most crucial environment for developing the next generation of great women. It's truly something to behold the development of something created from new life.

Society has shown the real way of defining or describing a wonderful woman. We have some ideas about what the particular aspect of womanhood really is, but we've lost the art of teaching it. So, this is my attempt to breakdown what I believe is how a wonderful woman is created. This Book is not meant to be the "best design or gospel" but give a good starting point of oral literature to begin a conversation of self-inspiring or inspiring others.

Table of Contents

History of Motherhood

History has proven the reality of what a woman does for society. Beyond the epic miracle of creating life. A woman has nurtured the world to be loving and caring with a mother's touch. This touch has developed households and community environments to the height of civility. We need to understand the real need for this important Mother, Woman, characteristic traits.

"To mother is to nurture, to train, to educate, to rear. As daughters of Eve, all women are uniquely gifted to help others in their lives become more."

Today we're losing this special trait to undeveloped and uneducated generations of women. The skill of Motherhood is no longer being taught to the new generation. There are many reasons that have impacted this downturn of this vital trait. The simple answer is past generations of women did not teach their next generation of women. We can look at a lot of causes that contributed to this downfall. But that would be blaming more than trying to correct the problem.

"Traditional: ideas and methods that have existed for a long time."

The purpose of this Book is to highlight all those positive traits and how they created and impacted a loving household and community environment. This new understanding of what value a woman that's taught and given these motherly traits can provide. This will cause the world to reevaluate the need to have a traditional woman in society. That shows the real effect that can only come from having real woman with Motherly traits. Not every woman will see the value or be willing to learn these traits. That doesn't mean we shouldn't try to teach the next generation of women those traits.

This duty to teach daughters, girls and young ladies is by no means an easy or lighthearted task. A long with different skills there are emotional components that adds a very touchy area for woman. That's why it must be taught to the next generation of women by a very experienced woman that has real life knowledge, like her mother. The very sensitive nature and emotional element of bearing a baby, controlling a household, and caring and loving a husband is a lot. These traits are not something that can be taught overnight, it's a lengthy process.

The process must be cultivated over the years of growth each girl, young lady and woman goes through for adulthood. This traditional woman concept is one of the most important aspects of building a family, and community. We need to emphasis and celebrate the role of the traditional woman in society. We can't let the value to our society that a well taught, prepared woman bring to the community be lessened. Our real society values will suffer if we lose this integral part of human life.

<u>Family Dynamic</u>

Present day we have lost the art and meaning of family. Parents are stewards of the next generation of Doctors, Lawyers, Mothers, and Political Leaders. They must take this responsibility seriously and do their duty as parents to raise the world's next generation. The first level of planning starts in the family household. It must be well coordinated and thought out to provide the best chance for the children to succeed. All aspects of the child's life should be planned and considered at each level.

"Mothers have such a high calling and privilege to teach the next generation of women."

The special responsibility that Mothers have in teaching their daughter how to be a woman is so very important that it can't be over emphasized. Society will surely breakdown if we lose the traditional trait of womanhood. Mother's must take up the mantal of teaching the next generation of woman how to be a **Homemaker, Wife, and Mother.** There is no scenario or situation that has our society moving forward without woman having those womanly traits. We must continue to create great mothers that cultivate our community to be civil and a peaceful place to live.

"Civil Society: distinct from government and business and including the family and private sphere."

The sacrifice a mother will endure to raise a daughter into a woman that's valuable enough to marry is worthy of praise. All the traits and skills a mother must teach are numerous. There are some more important than others, but all are necessary to complete the development. Like all areas in life some things are used more than others, but each have value. Everything we learn will one day come in handy to solve or work out a situation.

There is nowhere in the world that a woman taught in the traditional sense doesn't impact the daily routine of each community. She will provide that community with a much-needed woman component which allows the day to be normal. We may not be able to see what value and the immeasurable part of life that women produce. But make no mistake women put the order of life on the path for success. Men would be at a loss if women didn't do the Motherly duties in the family.

The Mother that I watched did her duties with pride and enthusiasm that taught my sisters all the aspects of being a woman. They learned each skill and trait which made them the great women that they are today. So, our family home environment was the key to their development.

Traits a Woman should have!

We all know that there is no such thing as a perfect person man or woman. But we can expect to find individuals that have specific desirable traits. Traits that have been taught to them from responsible parents that understand the value they provide. Women have a variety of traits that impact their ability to be chosen as a wife. So, the better they learn each trait and are able to display that emotion will be a deciding factor.

There are specific traits that may be more important than others like **"Feminine Traits,"** Grace, Radiance, **Resilience** to name a few. But each man might value their own set of traits that he feels fit the woman that he wants to start a family. Having been taught the meaning of many of these traits will provide a suitable knowledge base that can be a plus. Not being taught these traits will definitely be a negative detractor for men.

More Traits:

"Nurturance, sensitivity, sweetness, supportiveness, gentleness, warmth, passivity, cooperativeness, expressiveness, modesty, humility, empathy, affection, tenderness, and being emotional, kind, helpful, devoted, and understanding."

There can be countless other traits add to the list, but these should give you some idea as to what may constitute desirable feature for a man. Not to say that these are the only or most important to a man, he will have his own wants and needs to please or satisfy. The dynamic relationship between a man and a woman are very specific and sensitive. That why we as a society must ensure that the best options for men and women to choose from are available.

"Desirable: worth having or wanting; pleasing qualities."

Which means parents should do their due diligence and plan for their family to make the greatest possible outcome for the success of their children. We must stop playing ignorant of the fact that being in a relationship doesn't produce children. We run around with our heads in the clouds and are surprised that you have a baby on the way. This type of willful neglect has our communities on an unsustainable path moving towards doom.

Skills that are taught/handed down.

When I first watched and seen how my mother taught and showed my sisters what housework was about. I thought that it was punishment for them doing something wrong. So, I stayed far away from whatever area that they were in, so I didn't get caught up in the mix. I didn't realize that what my mother was teaching them would be very useful and important one day.

Then when she showed me some of the things that all adult men would need to know and use, it became obvious that it wasn't punishment. But they were very important skills that will make life much easier to live knowing those forever skills. When we're in the moment we can't understand the importance of performing those stupid and annoying tasks.

"Skills: knowledge, competencies, ability to do something well."

There is a lesson to learn from all the household chores that we must do on a daily basis. My gosha moment came when I was in the military and had to wash and iron my own clothes. What my mother had taught me came out so naturally that it was very reassuring to know that I had this ability. So, some of the most important skills that you'll need to function as a normal adult are below.

Basic Skills:

"House Cleaning, Washing Dishes/Clothes, Ironing Clothes, Sewing, Cooking, Baking, Hair Care, Skin Care, Dressing Attire, Proper Speaking Skills, Basic etiquette."

These skills are a small number of what women may learn during their development years. There are likely many cultural skills that women may get taught from their ethnic group, geographic location, and religious beliefs. The fact of knowing a simple skill like sewing to fix a window curtain or a girl's dress and a boy's pants is important. So, a woman's level of competence will be very evident from how she handles basic house chores. That why today's men are now being very chooses with the women they date.

The importance of those basic skills to be handed down to the next generation is paramount for the future. The critical skill of caring for a baby or infant child will have a real-life time effect on the community. We need to ensure that every generation can perform household basic skills to forge a great community. It is the responsibility of the parents to provide a safe learning environment in the home. If the next generation of women are not taught those traits and skills society will suffer from a smaller number of family being started.

<u>Duty of each Generation</u>

Society has evolved from the advancements created by each past generation. The mission of each past generation was to make society better than how they had it. Going from "out houses" to bathroom in the home. It's a simple proposition to change things that make life easier for the next generation. You would think that it a "No Brainer" to want your children to live better than you did.

"Duty: moral or legal obligation, a responsibility."

There has been a breakdown in specific communities to be more self-centered. This creates a mindset that the future generation will take care of themselves. We don't need to do anything to make life better for them, they can do it. Which has led to the destruction of communities that could be prosperous and healthy productive contributors.

The duties that mother have with raising their daughter are by no means simple. But they must take on the responsibility of teaching them all the womanly skills needed to build a home. There must be a new generation of women that can fill the position of **Homemaker, Wife, and Mother.** If we want the future of our society to succeed and be productive there must be competent and highly skilled women.

"Homemaker: manages a household as a spouse and parent."
"Wife: woman you're willing to spend the rest of your life with and raise a family."
"Mother: woman in relation to her child or children with care and affection."

We need to make a conscious effort to change the direction of our communities. Get back to the basics and teach the next generation of women their much-needed contribution. Our only hope is to take prompt action and show the value of those womanly skills. Let the next generation know how difunctional life will be without their individual contribution.

"Contribution: something that help to achieve a goal."

They must also be taught the wonderful and unbelievable sense of pride knowing you created a home that is filled with endless levels of unconditional love. The home they have built is a tribute to their competence and skill level to be a **Homemaker, Wife, and Mother.** This world will be a better place to live because of the home environment that permeates through the community.

<u>Why is it necessary to</u>
<u>continue this tradition?</u>

If the "Human Race" is not willing to pass on life sustaining skills that provide comfort to everyday living. Then what the meaning of being "Human?" Not being able to leave the world in a better place would be a sad state of affairs. People are gifted with a unique skill that sets us apart from every other living thing on earth.

"Sustainment: capacity of a system to endure, keep in existence, maintain and preserve life."

Not leaving a heritage that helps the next generation create, build, produce, and modernize the community would be maddest. This would make our environment no better than that of the "Animal Kingdom." We need to provide as people all the necessary skills that allow the next generation to thrive. There are no skills that are less useful than other skills, they all have a place in our community.

"Heritage: important parts of society's history and culture."

There is nothing more important than the miracle of life that a woman can create. Having the ability to nurture and cultivate a child is one of the greatest wonders in this world. The woman role in our society is so precious that we can't allow that ability to be lost to ideal thoughts. We must ensure that the next generation is filled with women that have the skills of, **"Homemakers, Wives, and Mothers."** This would enable our heritage and culture to continue to exist with the world becoming a better place to live.

How a Woman conduct Herself!

It said that if you don't learn from history then you are doomed to repeat it. History gives us many examples of how the "Human Race" has advanced. Creating better ways to live comfortably and support life. There is no great example then what the woman population has provided. Their achievements revolve around creating a "Nuclear Household" that provides the world with the next great leader, doctor, lawyer, and mother.

"Conduct: manner in which a person behaves."

The way in which women conduct themselves in a direct reflection on how well she was taught. Society has afforded the woman population to become more independent and given the ability to choices her direction. This has now led to a dysfunctional generation of women with no clear understanding of their responsibility. Not teaching or passing on the very important skills being a **"Homemaker, Wife, and Mother"** is criminal.

"Reflection: process of accessing information to create, invoke a mental process of critical thinking and problem solving."

Women today have no idea about the precious heritage that has been lost on them. There was a uniqueness that woman personified when they learn the traditional skills and displayed that characteristic daily. Men were intrigue and drawn to women that show her femininity with pride. Proud to be considered a woman worthy of wanting with pleasing qualities.

"Personified: embodiment attributed to human nature, vivid image."

The new culture of no standard and no accountability for your actions is a disgrace to the past generation of hard-working men and women. These disrespectful individuals have started to erode our society from the inside out. The more we let them continue to live without proper manners and respect the worse it will get.

"Biological: pertaining to life and living things."

For women to uphold the tradition of being a proper lady is not asking for too much. It's a biological trait that's given to women for rearing and caring for children and a husband. This is the natural process of human existence that must be continued in order to protect the future. Everyone needs to take part in preparing the next generation to be successful.

A Women's Attitude.

There are a lot of reasons that women should be feeling some kind of way about their reality. They should also be given praise for dealing with it for all these years. I would be the first to say that they have been mistreated. But I would also say that the world has a specific design and was made that way for a logical reason. That logical and spiritual reason was to appropriate life on this planet to continue human existence.

"Attitude: set of emotions, beliefs, and behaviors toward a particular object, person, thing, or event."

If we allow society to keep traveling down this unsustainable path, we only have a few more decades to live on earth. We must make a change now to correct our direction and change course to a better future. It all starts with the attitude and mindset of woman to spark the change. Every mother and would be mother must make the conscious effort to do their duty and teach the next generation of **Homemakers, Wives, and Mothers.**

"Mindset: a person's way of feeling, thinking, acting, and their opinion."

There has been a grand plan to disrupt specifically targeted communities. One of the ways it's been done is through the uneducated population in each community. The best place to start is with each community's life bears the woman. This is a whole discussion for another book. The design is to create the faults belief that women don't need a man. Then support this theory with just enough to create a livable situation.

"Community: social group of diverse people living in the same place."

The next step was to instill a mindset that they don't need to follow anyone rules. They can just live however they please without the control a stable home would provide. A stable home would allow them to live with personal restraint and a proper mindset. Living in a volatile home environment would contribute to the downfall of the community.

"Stable Home: support family well-being and lower stress levels."

The biggest part of this situation is the attitude or mindset of the modern woman. If they could just see the corrupt trap that was planned for them to fall into and work their way out. This world would have a chance to correct what has been happening and build a better society. We needed the woman to want to take on this monumental and very important task to save the world.

<u>Conclusion</u>

As we look around the world and observe the behavior that is being displayed. No one can deny that things are getting out of hand. There are women that act without caring about what their action may do to another person. This careless attitude must be put back in check and corrected with a harish responses. We must let all women in society know you will be held responsible for your conduct.

This Book is my attempt to put a spotlight on the need for women to take an active part in correcting this downward spiral of the behavior in some women. This small number of pages highlights what I believe is a slow erosion of society norms. Those behavior norms and mannerisms that make humanity the apex society on earth. If we don't act to change this situation life may be on its way to destruction.

If men are not given a reason or worthy women to pursue there may be no need to continue creating a wonderful world. Men want something to work for and spend their life trying to create the prefect household. The most valuable thing that can make a man work his heart out is a woman. That why society needs to produce quality women worthy of being wanted.

www.ingramcontent.com/pod-product-compliance
Lightning Source LLC
Chambersburg PA
CBHW020922140626
46545CB00015B/1227